MORTIMER'S PORTRAIT ON GLASS

"Oh, please, Pa, can't we go in one of those," begged Arabel. "I've always wanted to live in a caravan. And so has Mortimer, haven't you, Mortimer?"

"Kaaark," said Mortimer.

Mortimer, of course, is Arabel's Raven.

The Joneses were looking at the horse-drawn caravans in the town of Ballyshoe. Even Mrs Jones thought a horse-drawn caravan would be a romantic way to see Ireland.

Soon they were ambling through the countryside at two miles an hour while Arabel read aloud to Mortimer. It was lovely and peaceful, until Mortimer said the only other word he could utter: "Nevermore!"

With Mortimer, nothing stays peaceful for long. Another madcap story of an established Jackanory favourite.

Joan Aiken

MORTIMER'S PORTRAIT ON GLASS

As told in Jackanory

illustrated by Quentin Blake

BBC/KNIGHT BOOKS

Copyright © Joan Aiken Enterprises Ltd 1982
Illustrations © Quentin Blake 1982
First published 1982 by the
British Broadcasting Corporation/Knight Books.

British Library C.I.P.

Aiken, Joan
    Mortimer's portrait on glass.—(Knight books)
    I. Title   II. Blake, Quentin
    823'.914[J]   PZ7

ISBN 0-340-27534-0
    (0 563 17883 3 BBC)

Printed and bound in Great Britain for
the British Broadcasting Corporation,
35 Marylebone High Street, London W1M 4AA
and Hodder and Stoughton Paperbacks, a
division of Hodder and Stoughton Ltd,
Mill Road, Dunton Green, Sevenoaks,
Kent (Editorial Office: 47 Bedford
Square, London, WC1 3DP) by
Richard Clay (The Chaucer Press) Ltd,
Bungay, Suffolk. Photoset by
Rowland Phototypesetting Ltd,
Bury St Edmunds, Suffolk.

1

"Do you want to know about laser beams, Mortimer?" asked Arabel.

"Kaaark," said Mortimer.

So far as he was concerned, Arabel might as well have asked if he wanted to know about exports of methylated spirit from Westphalia. Mortimer was not interested in laser beams. All he wanted to do was to annoy the horse, Katie Daley, so much that she would break into a gallop. In pursuance of this aim, he was pelting Katie's fat brown back with cherry-stones. Katie was taking no notice whatsoever; but after three or four of the stones had hit Mr Jones, who was leading the horse, on the back of his head, he turned round and shouted: "Stop that, Mortimer, or I won't half give you a sorting!"

The Jones family were travelling through Ireland in a horse-drawn caravan, on their way to visit Great-aunt Rosie Ryan.

Where, you may ask, was Mr Jones's taxi? It had developed clutch trouble as they reached a little town called Ballyshoe. A new clutch had been ordered, but it was going to take five days, since it had to be fetched from the other side of the country. And while this was being discussed, Arabel had noticed a whole row of horse-drawn caravans standing in the main square of Ballyshoe, waiting to be hired.

"Oh, *please*, Pa, can't we go on in one of those?" she begged, pulling at her father's sleeve. "I've *always* wanted to live in a caravan. And so has Mortimer, haven't you, Mortimer?"

"Kaaark," said Mortimer.

"And it would be much better than waiting here for a week while the taxi is fixed. We could go on and see Great-aunt Rosie and then come back here and pick up the taxi. Couldn't we, Ma?"

"That's ever such a sensible idea, really,

Ben," said Mrs Jones. "And it would be *ever* so romantic, travelling in one of them gypsyfied waggonettes: a real Romanesque holiday."

"Oh, very well, very well," grumbled Mr Jones, when they had gone on at him for a while. "But it's against my better judgment, mind! Those things only go about two miles an hour. And who's going to look after the horse, may I ask? You don't just pour oil and petrol into a horse, you got to brush them and comb them and curry them and I don't know what-all.''

"I daresay it's ever so easy, really,'' said Mrs Jones. "They'll tell us about the curry at the hiring office; probably give you a big box of it there like those do-it-yourself curry kits they got in the windows of Indian grocers."

"*I'll* do the brushing," said Arabel eagerly. "I'd *like* to do it."

"Supposing its shoes need changing?" said Mr Jones.

Arabel was surprised. "Mustn't horses get their feet wet?" she said.

"No, but sometimes they drop their shoes in the road."

"Oh well, Mortimer will keep a look-out for that, won't you, Mortimer?"

"Kaaark," said Mortimer.

So here the Joneses were, travelling at two miles an hour towards Great-aunt Rosie in Castlecoffee. (They had phoned her and said they might be a few days later than expected.)

At present their road lay across a huge brown bog which was called Black Feakle's Slough. As far as the eye could see there was nothing but flatness and brownness. Arabel had wanted to come this way because she had heard that there was a dinosaur's footprint on a small hill, right in the middle

of the bog. She had always wanted to see a
dinosaur's footprint. But now even Arabel
was getting a little bored with the brown
view; she was sitting on the steps of the
caravan, as it rolled slowly along, reading
aloud to Mortimer out of the *Children's
Encyclopedia*. Mortimer wasn't listening. Mrs
Jones was taking a nap inside the caravan.

And Mr Jones was leading the horse, Katie
Daley, along the road, because if he did not,
she tended to come to a dead stop and begin
eating the stringy clumps of heather by the
roadside.

"I *knew* it would work out like this,"
muttered Mr Jones from time to time. "Oh,
my fallen arches!"

His daughter had offered to lead the
horse, but Katie Daley was so large, and
Arabel was so small, that she was not able to
reach the reins.

"*Why* do you suppose a dinosaur stepped
on the hill in the middle of Black Feakle's
Slough, Pa?" she called.

"Wanted to get out of here fast, I
daresay," grumbled Mr Jones. "And I don't
blame him. This place is as flat as the
perishing Siberian desert. *And* as cold."

It *was* cold. Arabel was wearing two
sweaters. Mortimer had his feathers all
puffed out. People they met along the road
said it was the coldest summer since the
French landed in Ireland, and that was over
a hundred and ninety years ago. Icy winds
were blowing down from the North Pole,
and these were the cause of the unseasonable
weather.

Katie Daley threw her head about so much, and whinnied so loudly, that Mr Jones buckled her night-blanket round her. Arabel hugged Mortimer tightly, so that they could use each other's warmth, and went on teaching him about laser beams.

"Laser beams are made of light, Mortimer," she said. "Scientists have managed to squeeze a whole slab of light together into a thin stick like a knitting-needle. And it is so sharp that it can cut through steel, or sew up people's eyes if they have holes in them."

"Nevermore!" said Mortimer, very amazed.

"If *we* had a laser beam we could stitch Katie Daley's shoes back on, Pa," Arabel said, "if they came off."

"Huh! I'd like to see a laser beam in this perishing wilderness," muttered Mr Jones.

"I wish we did have one. Maybe we could use it to fry up a few chips and onions. I'm sick to death of baked beans."

Just at that moment, Mortimer, whose sight was very keen, noticed something in the far distance, and let out a croak.

"What is it, Mortimer?" said Arabel. "Can you see a dinosaur?"

"Nevermore," said Mortimer. He began to struggle in Arabel's arms, and finally jumped down into the road, and flapped off sideways across the blackish-brown spongy peat.

"Watch it, Mortimer!" called Mr Jones. "You sink into the bog, no one's going to pull you out! And I mean that! I'm not risking my neck for no raven!"

However the weather lately had been so cold and dry that the bog was not very boggy any more; or at least not round the edges. It was like a bouncy brown mattress.

"Mortimer, please come back!" called Arabel anxiously.

But Mortimer went on walking across the bog. (He never flew if he could help it.) So

Arabel jumped down from the caravan steps and went after him.

"Arabel, dearie! Just you come right back here!" called Mr Jones.

But Arabel went on picking her way after Mortimer.

"I believe he has seen a dinosaur!" she called back to her father. "There's something kicking and splashing out there in the bog!"

Mr Jones looped Katie Daley's reins round her front legs to discourage her from going on without him (which, however, she was not at all inclined to do) and began making his way gingerly after his daughter and raven, carrying the driving whip with him, just in case.

"*Arabel!*" he shouted crossly. "Where the blazes do you think you're going?"

"But look, Pa," Arabel shouted back, "there *is* something over there, a dinosaur or something, flapping about and carrying on."

"Well, I'm sure I hope it isn't one of those Bog People," said Mr Jones. "You never know *what* you're going to come across in a back-of-beyond spot like this. I wish to goodness we'd never *come* this godforsaken way, that I do! Anyway it's as well I brought the whip along; I can always use the handle to punch whatever it is in the snout. Arabel! *Mortimer! Will* you come back out of there?"

"No, Pa, listen!" said Arabel. "I can hear somebody calling *help, help!*"

Now even Mr Jones began to think he could see something. "I bet it's a black boggart," he muttered. "Or one of them perishing leprechauns they're always on about. Leprechauns! I'd make 'em lep!"

But then *he* began to hear the voice calling *help, help!* "Bless my soul! If it isn't some silly bloke what's got stuck in the bog! But what in the world did he go *out* there for? That's what I'd like to know? He must be dicked in the nob! Don't you go getting too close to him, now, Arabel, ducky. You can feel it's getting real unreliable underfoot."

Indeed, the spongy-brown mattress had turned to something more like half-cooked toffee, or chocolate fudge that has not set properly. Arabel was up to her knees in it.

"*I* think it's a man, Pa!" she shouted to Mr Jones. "He must be right up to his waist in the bog. Why don't you throw him the end of your whip, and then we can pull him out by the handle?"

This seemed a good suggestion to Mr Jones. The whip was a long leather thong, fastened to a thick, strong, wooden handle.

Standing on the firmest bit of ground he could find, a sort of lumpy tussock, Mr Jones hurled the thong of his whip forward, like a fisherman casting a line.

But the bitter cold wind was blowing so strongly from the other direction that it kept blowing the thong back to him again.

"Dang it! Plague take the perishing thing!" muttered Mr Jones. "*Now* what's to do? *Arabel!* Will you come back out of that goo? You're up to your knees already. What your Ma will say when she sees you, I do not know!"

"Glup! Gwilp!" shouted the man in the bog. He seemed to have mud in his mouth.

Then Arabel had another good idea. "Mortimer! Could you very kindly take the end of the whiplash in your beak and fly with it over to that person in the bog?"

She spoke as persuadingly as she knew how. Normally, Mortimer was the last bird in the world to do anybody a favour; he was not interested in other people's troubles. But fortunately, just now, he happened to be quite curious about the black, thrashing

creature in the bog. So, after thinking about
it for a long minute or two, he opened his
beak, jammed the end of the whiplash in it,
shut his beak again, and set off in a slow,
reluctant, grumbling manner to fly the
twelve feet or so across the bog. When he
was directly over the stuck person he began
to hover on his wings like a hawk, and
dropped the end of the line.

"Oh, well *done*, Mortimer!" called Arabel,
very pleased indeed, because she had not
been at all sure that Mortimer would be
inclined to help.

The muddy person grabbed the line, and Mr Jones began to pull on the whiphandle with all his strength. But for a while it seemed quite hopeless: like trying to drag up a cast-iron manhole-cover with a spiderweb. Arabel went to help her father; she, too, seized hold of the whip-handle and began to tug and strain. Nothing happened at all.

Mortimer, flying round and round above the person in the bog, now decided to take a hand; or rather, a claw.

Swooping down, he grabbed a clawful of something, snatched a beakful of the bogged person, all he could see sticking out of the mud, and then gave a mighty flap upwards, shouting "*Nevermore!*" at the top of his voice. There was an equally loud yell from the person in the bog, and a tremendous explosion of mud, froth, and peaty water. Arabel and her father both sat down violently on the brown squashy ground, as the line suddenly shot backwards towards them.

"Don't let go! Keep on pulling, dearie!" shouted Mr Jones, scrambling to his feet again, and he gave another powerful jerk on the whip-handle.

Now the person on the other end of the line came right out of the bog, with a loud, sucking, squelching slop! and began crawling and sliding towards Arabel and Mr Jones as they hauled on the line.

"Rare good whips they make in these parts, I'll give 'em that," grunted Mr Jones, pulling away. "And just as well too, with all these-here perishing bogs about."

Mortimer, mad with excitement, was flapping around the person's head, making grabs at his hair and collar and ears;

hindering, in fact, rather more than he helped. They heard a frantic shout: "Will ye be getting that godforsaken bird off me before he has the eyes out of my head entirely?"

"Mortimer!" panted Arabel. "I think you'd better come back to us."

Mortimer seemed quite unwilling to do so – he was really interested in the rescue operation by this time – but luckily, next minute, they had managed to drag the bogfast person on to a bit of ground that was firm enough for him to stand upright, and he did so.

Now they could see that it was a man, though he was covered with dark-brown treacly goo from head to foot.

"Kaaark!" said Mortimer, very disgusted indeed to find it was only a human they had rescued, and not a dinosaur. He was so annoyed that he shrugged his wings, let go of the man's ear (which he had been grasping in his beak), flopped heavily on to the ground, and began walking slowly and sulkily back to the caravan, kicking away

bits of peaty soil with his rear toes at every
step.

"Begorrah!" said the man they had
rescued, wiping the black slime from his
eyes. "Ye've saved me life, between ye, but
I'm thinking it may have been at the cost of

25

my ears! Yon carrion crow, or whatever he
is, has notched them like postage stamps."
And he rubbed them ruefully, adding: "Still,
I'm not complaining. I'd have been a goner!
I'm greatly obliged to the pair of ye!"

"What in the name of nonsense were you
doing out there on the bog?" inquired Mr
Jones rather indignantly, as they all began to
pick their way with care back towards the
road.

"Ah, well, ye see, I'm an entomologist in
my spare time – that's a bug-hunter to you,
acushla," said the man to Arabel. "And I'd
heard tell of a colony of the Large Pink

Butterfly out on Feakle's Slough – very rare
the Large Pink is now, almost extinct – so,
seeing the bog's uncommonly dry this
season, I thought I'd try my luck.''

"And did you see any?" inquired Arabel,
greatly interested.

"I'd a glimpse of some, alannah, I believe,
but they were a great way off yet. 'Tis a
shame I couldn't get closer to them before I
began to sink."

Slowly and gingerly, the three of them
drew nearer Katie Daley, the caravan, and
Mrs Jones.

27

2

Mrs Jones had been enjoying a nap inside
the caravan, but Mortimer's annoyed
croaking and flapping on the roof above her
had woken her up. When she looked out and
saw the three black figures approaching out
of the bog – for Mr Jones and Arabel had
also been fairly smothered in mud during the
course of the rescue – Mrs Jones let out such
a screech that even Katie Daley pricked up
her ears and lifted her head from the scrubby
bunch of roadside heather that she was
chewing.

"*Merciful cats alive! Murder!* It's three
Gypsy Mummies come out of the bog to cut
our throats! Help, help! Ben! Arabel! Where
are you? It's Black Feakle himself, risen from
his watery tomb – or Black Treacle – and
brought two of his fiendish lepidoptera along
with him. Help, help! Ben, Arabel, where
are you?"

"It's all right, Ma, it's us!" called Arabel reassuringly. "We pulled a man out of the bog. He's not a Gypsy Mummy, his name is Mr Plunkett."

For on the walk back to the road the rescued man told Mr Jones that, when not chasing butterflies, he was a respectable factory owner, and lived not far off in the port town of Glasshaven.

When Mrs Jones finally realised that it was her husband and child who were coming out of the bog with a stranger, looking like three mud-covered Guy Fawkeses, she was hardly less horrified.

"Oh, my poor palpitating heart! How do you *ever* expect to get all that washed off, tell me that, when there's only one little pink basin in the caravan no bigger than a salad bowl! I can't shut my eyes for *five minutes* but you're into some mischief Arabel Jones, and your father's just as bad! I don't know, I'm sure it's enough to give a body the historical fantods just to *look* at you – I believe I feel one of my spasms coming on!"

"Ah, now, let ye be easy, ma'am," said Mr Plunkett kindly. "Ye must all come back to Glasshaven with me and have a grand wash-up at my place – I've two bathrooms and all the hot water in the world. And my housekeeper will be after making a bundle of your muddy things and taking them round to the laundrette. Sure, it's clean as mushrooms your husband and daughter will be in no time at all, missis, and I invite ye all to stay and have dinner in my house tonight, and I'll be showing ye round my factory."

This seemed like a friendly and hospitable plan, but Mr Jones inquired cautiously, "How far will it be to Glasshaven, Mr Plunkett?"

"Glory be, 'tis nothing of a distance! Twenty miles, if that. And my own car parked a step of the way along the road, I could be taking the lady in it if she wishes."

"*Twenty miles?*" said Mr Jones. "Katie Daley won't do that in two days."

But, to his amazement, Mr Plunkett unwound the reins from Katie's forefeet, snapped them briskly along her fat back, and shouted, "Musha, now, will ye!" in such a commanding voice that Katie instantly set off at a gallop, almost before Mr Jones and Arabel had time to scramble on board the caravan.

Mortimer fell backwards off the roof and was quite cross because he had to flap his fastest in order to catch up again. However once he was safely inside he began to enjoy the breakneck pace very much, and yelled with pleasure and excitement, jumping up and down a great many times on one of the well-sprung bunks.

"Yonder's the dinosaur's footprint!" called Mr Plunkett, as they dashed past a little hill in the middle of the bog. On one of its sloping rocky sides could plainly be seen a set of marks like those made by six enormous toes.

"I wish I could see a dinosaur," Arabel sighed wistfully. "Look, Mortimer, here's a picture of one in the encyclopedia. It was eighty feet long and weighed fifty tons."

"Have one of those for Sunday dinner, you'd be eating shepherds' pie for weeks," said Mrs Jones.

Now they came to Mr Plunkett's car, parked by the side of the road where he'd left it to go in quest of Large Pink Butterflies. Mr Jones was fairly sure that he would never be able to persuade Katie Daley to gallop, so he got into the car and drove it, while Mr Plunkett continued to act as coachman for the caravan. In not much more than an hour they had crossed a row of grassy hills, and could see the sea ahead of them. Soon they reached a small harbour town.

"That's my factory," said Mr Plunkett proudly, pointing to a long, grey stone building.

"What does it make?" asked Arabel. But Mr Plunkett was not paying attention. He was staring out to sea and exclaiming: "Glory be to goodness, and isn't that an iceberg drifting towards the shore? Or am I

not to be believing the evidence of me own two eyes? True 'tis the coldest summer since the French landed, but I never did see an iceberg so close to land at this season of the year!"

However it was quite evident that he *could* believe the evidence of his eyes and that it *was* an iceberg. It floated about a mile out to sea – a great green mountain of ice – and a whole lot of people from Glasshaven were crowded on the grassy cliffs and harbour-side, watching it with great admiration.

"Wurra! Yerrah! Musha!" they were all saying. "Did ye ever see the like?"

"Look, Mortimer, just look!" said Arabel.

"Nevermore!" said Mortimer wonderingly. He had never seen an iceberg in his life. Nor, for that matter, had Arabel.

However it was too cold to stay on the dockside, all wet and muddy as they were. Mr Plunkett took the Jones family to his house so that Arabel and her father could get washed and change out of their muddy clothes. There were two huge bathrooms, one blue, the other green; even Mortimer was pleased to take a shower, which shot out a sideways jet like the wake of a hydrofoil. Meanwhile Katie Daley was turned loose in the paddock with Mr Plunkett's sorrel pony and a bag of oats; and Mr Plunkett, as soon as he, too, had put on clean clothes, began to

35

bustle about like mad, getting the garden
boy to take the Joneses' clothes to the
laundrette, and urging his housekeeper to
cook a feast for the preservers who had saved
him from the bog.

"While it's cooking I'll show ye over my
factory, and we'll be taking another look at
the iceberg for it's a grand sight entirely, and
not one ye'd be likely to see where ye live in
London," he said. "Don't forget, now, Mrs
O'Hegarty, the boxsty, the dillisk, the stelk,
the frumenty, and the carrageen moss!"

When Arabel and her father were dry and
warm, and Mortimer had been persuaded to
come out of the shower, and Mrs Jones had
put on some lipstick and a headscarf and her
thickest jacket, they all walked back to the
factory which was on the harbour-side. By
the water it seemed even colder; a freezing
breeze blew towards them from the iceberg,
which was drifting in with the tide, coming
closer and closer to land.

Arabel (and Mortimer) would have
preferred to stay on the wharf and watch the
iceberg, but Mrs Jones said, "Come along,

dearie; it's perishing out here; and if Mr Plunkett is so kind as to show us his factory, it's not polite to loiter outside."

"What does the factory make, Mr Plunkett?" Arabel asked again.

But Mr Plunkett and her father had walked on ahead, and she received no answer to her question. Mrs Jones gave her hand a tug, to hurry her on, and, coming up with the two men in front, Arabel heard Mr Plunkett say: "In the old days, of course, they used diamonds to cut the designs, but now we are more up-to-date and use laser beams."

"*Laser beams?*" said Arabel, very interested. "What do you use laser beams for, Mr Plunkett?"

But Mr Plunkett did not hear her. He was hurrying Mr Jones inside the factory, eager to show him all his work. "That's right, that's right, come along with ye," he said, holding a big door open for Mrs Jones to follow, and Arabel, with Mortimer sitting on her shoulder.

By now it was well after tea-time, and the

sun was low in the western sky, shining in sideways through the factory windows, which were very large and clear. As they came into the main workshop, Arabel gave a gasp, and so did Mrs Jones, who quickly dived a hand into her pink raffia handbag, found her sunglasses, and clapped them on her nose. For there was such a flashing and a sparkling, such a shining dazzling spangling bright shimmering luminousness all about that, for several minutes, the visitors could see hardly anything whatsoever; all they could do was stand and blink.

"Kaaark!" whispered Mortimer.

"Blow me!" said Mr Jones.

"Oh, Mortimer, isn't it *beautiful!*" said Arabel.

But just the same she was a little anxious. She held tightly on to Mortimer's leg, in case he should do anything rash. For Mr Plunkett's factory was a glass factory.

There were cut-glass tumblers, and salad bowls, and great wide punch-bowls, and tiny liqueur glasses, and great round brandy

glasses like balloons, there were glass plates
and glass clocks and shimmering rows of
glass wind-bells like organ pipes, there were
rose bowls and wine glasses, there were
cut-glass perfume flasks and powder-bowls
and delicately twisted long-stemmed
flower-holders, there were glass finger-bowls
and pitchers and goblets and candle-sticks.
The light from the setting sun caught all the
edges of the cut-glass and threw millions of
different-coloured sparks all over
everywhere, rose and green and tangerine,
blue and purple and orange and
lemon-yellow. Arabel had purple freckles all
over her face, Mortimer had a lemon-yellow
waistcoat. And the smooth glass all around
them shimmered and shone and dazzled like
a whole forest full of decorated Christmas
trees!

Arabel thought she had never seen anything so gorgeous. She was still nervous about Mortimer, and held tight on to his leg, but she couldn't help being interested, as Mr Plunkett began telling Mr Jones how they cut the patterns on the cut-glass with a laser beam.

"Where do you keep your laser beam, Mr Plunkett?" she asked.

"Bless your heart, and isn't it a fair caution you are, and as interested and sensible as a grown person!" said Mr Plunkett. "The laser beam lives here in this big box like a giant camera on a turntable,

see, and we put a bit of glassware in the jaws here, like this, see, and then switch on the beam – you can alter the power, for thick glass or thin glass, like this – and then you can write a pattern on a glass, easy as with a pencil on a piece of paper. Look now, acushla, I'll guide your hand and then you can write your name on the glass – this is the way of it."

So, with great care, and only a little wiggly, Arabel wrote *Arabel*

on a tumbler, and Mortimer, breathing heavily, leaned over her shoulder and watched.

"Oh please, now can I draw a picture of Mortimer on another glass?" said Arabel. "He *would* like that."

"Arabel! It's rude to ask!" interrupted Mrs Jones, but Mr Plunkett said: "Sure, indeed, and ye can," and tucked another glass into the jaws of the machine. These were covered with velvet to prevent the glass from slipping out.

Arabel had drawn pictures of Mortimer so often that it was very easy for her to trace an outline of his big hairy beak, his feathery wings, his bootbutton eyes, his long tail, his untidy trousers, and his sharp, horny claws.

"There!" she said. "There you are, Mortimer, on the glass!"

Mortimer looked over Arabel's shoulder and saw his portrait cut on the glass. And, at that, he was so amazed that, without even intending to, he did something that caused an absolutely tremendous amount of damage.

He drew a deep breath and yelled out: "NEVERMORE!" at the top of his terrifically loud, hoarse, croaking voice.

A high note played on a violin can shatter a drinking-glass. And a blast blown on a trumpet can knock down a wall. And a peal of bells can break a mirror. And, in exactly the same way, Mortimer's shout of *Nevermore* shattered every single piece of glass in the workshop. Fragments and splinters fell about everywhere; sparks twinkled and shards tinkled; never was such a clinking and clanking, flashing and crashing, glittering and scrunching and scintillating

and spangling and jangling, chiming,
jingling and twangling.

"Holy Moses!" said Mr Plunkett.

And all his workmen were saying similar
things:

"Bejabers!"

"Glory be to goodness!"

"Mercy on us!"

"Begorrah!"

"Who'd ha' thought it?"

"Did you ever, in all your livelong days,
see anything to equal that?"

"Sure and the bird must be the very divil
himself!"

3

"Oh, Mortimer!" said Arabel. "*Look* what you've done!"

Even Mortimer was quite startled and abashed. He gazed around him at the sparkling wreckage with his big blackberry eyes; he muttered to himself thoughtfully, and poked with his claw at a fragment of shining glass that happened to be lying nearby.

The only article in the whole place still remaining unbroken, as it happened, was the tumbler on which Arabel had drawn Mortimer's picture. That was still clasped in the velvet jaws of the laser machine.

Mrs Jones gulped. Mr Jones had turned quite pale.

"Oh dear," he began.

"Ah, now, don't ye be giving it a single thought," said Mr Plunkett quickly. "Sure

and the bird meant no harm. He doesn't
know his own potentiality! 'Tis my own fault
for fetching a raven into a glass factory; all
the world knows ravens are unchancy birds.
Bless ye, the insurance will be paying for it;
do not yez be worrying your heads about this
little mishap at all!''

Just the same, the horrified Jones family
felt that the best thing they could do was to
get out of the factory, and the town of
Glasshaven, and be on their way.

"I'll – I'll leave you my London address,
Mr Plunkett," said Mr Jones hoarsely,
"and – when you've reckoned up the cost of
the damage, you'll be so kind as to let me
know the total –"

But at this moment everybody was
distracted by one of the glassblowers! He
came rushing into the workshop, calling out:
"Will ye all be casting a look at the iceberg
now! And it drifting clean into the harbour!
And, begorrah, it has a great beast inside it,
like a starfish in a paperweight! Yerrah, 'tis
the greatest sight this town has seen since
the French landed!"

At this everybody (scrunching over the
piles and drifts of broken glass on the floor),
ran to the big factory windows to stare out
over the paved wharfside and the oval
harbour between its two arms of grassy cliff.

"Faith!" said Mr Plunkett. "Did ye ever
see the like? 'Tis like a ship in a bottle. 'Tis

like a chick in a glass egg! 'Tis like a nut in a
shell! 'Tis like a stone in a plum! What
manner of creature might that be, at all,
then? Sure, and its tail is longer than the
race-track at Fairyhouse, and its neck almost
as long! How can the poor beast be carrying
them two great appendages, now, answer me
that? 'Tis no wonder at all it got frozen up in
a hunk of ice, and best it stays there, I
reckon. Do you suppose it is still living in
there, the creature? Frozen alive, maybe, like
a winter fish in a lough?"

Mr Plunkett watched the landward
progress of the iceberg with considerable
anxiety: "Live or dead," he said, "if that
chunk of ice isn't halted before it hits our
dockside, there'll be little left of the port of
Glasshaven, or this factory either! What yon
bird achieved will be but a pennyworth of
damage compared with this one!"

At these words of warning, everybody
began to look very worried indeed. For,
although the iceberg was slipping along so
smoothly, now that it was inside the
harbour, everybody could see how very fast

it was moving. It grazed, bumpingly, along
the left-hand sea wall and scrunched up
half-a-dozen small boats like snail-shells.

"Och, mercy on us, what'll we ever do at
all?" somebody wailed. "If that hits the
town, every soul in it'll be turned to
meat-paste!"

"Mortimer! I believe that's a dinosaur in
there!" whispered Arabel. "See its long tail
and its long neck! Oh, don't you wish that
somebody would break the iceberg and let it
out?"

"Nevermore," muttered Mortimer, a little doubtfully, and he cast a wistful glance at the laser machine, where the wonderful glass with his picture on it still nestled between the velvet jaws.

It was then that Arabel had her good idea.

"Mr Plunkett!" she said timidly. "Don't you think that perhaps the laser machine could break the iceberg?"

"Glory be on high, 'tis pure genius that's in the child entirely," roared Mr Plunkett, and he dashed back to the laser box, spun it round until it was pointing towards the window, shouted, "Duck, everybody!" switched the volume up to full power, and directed the beam straight towards the approaching iceberg.

There was a moment of hush while everybody held their breath.

First the window melted and curled up like tissue-paper on a hot fire.

Then, with a majestic, grating, squeaking, crunching rumpus, like the sound of a branch splitting off a tree (only a million times more so), the iceberg fell in half.

"Oh, the dinosaur!" cried Arabel in dismay.

For the dinosaur, freed from its container, had sunk stiffly into the deep water of the bay, and disappeared.

Now Mr Plunkett was rapidly running his laser beam back and forth over the two halves of the iceberg, chopping them into smaller and smaller bits – rather like Mrs Jones making breadcrumbs before baking one of her apple-crumbles.

"There! Thanks be to providence and the child's good thinking, now we can all rest easy," Mr Plunkett said, turning down the power at last and switching off the laser beam. "Tom Foyle the harbourmaster and his lads can be dealing with the rest of the ice that's bobbing around; they can be towing it out to sea with the lifeboat, or packing it away in sawdust for next summer's ice-cream – if anybody in this town will ever have the heart to consume an ice-cream again!"

Certainly it seemed improbable that anybody would feel like ice-cream for a long, long time. The air in Glasshaven was so cold, from the closeness of the iceberg, that all the water had frozen in the pipes, and a small shower of rain had decided to turn to snow.

But nobody minded that.

"Well! Sure and we laid on a fine diversion for your first visit to Glasshaven!" Mr Plunkett said to the Joneses. "Now you must be coming back to my house for a warming drop of something; and I'm sure by this time Mrs O'Hegarty will be ready to dish up the boxsty and the dillisk and the stelk and the frumenty."

"Oh, but Mr Plunkett – the dinosaur!" said Arabel urgently. "Don't you think somebody ought to fish the poor thing up out of the water?"

"Alannah, that dinosaur has been frozen inside that iceberg for more million years

than you have fingers," Mr Plunkett said.
"And toes, too, likely. It won't hurt him at
all to wait at the bottom of our fine clean
harbour for a little. For the matter of that,
it'd be a rare, strong line that was capable of
fishing him up – 'twould need more than a
length of whiplash for that one! Let him
wait. And now I'm sure you all want your
dinner – as I do mine. Let you be coming
this way now."

All the way up the wide, sloping, main
street of Glasshaven, Arabel kept looking
wistfully back at the waters of the harbour.
And so she was the first to see the dinosaur
heave itself out of the water and step over the
cliff-top. She thought it was like watching a
horse climb out of a hand-basin – there
seemed so much dinosaur and so little water.

The great legs stepped over the cliff as if it were no higher than a matchbox, and the wash caused by the great tail caused a kind of tidal slop along the harbour front.

"Oh, Mortimer," breathed Arabel for the second time that day, "isn't it beautiful!"

"Errrk," said Mortimer thoughtfully. Even he found the dinosaur rather large.

It was a greenish-grey, very wrinkled, its hind-legs were bigger than its fore-legs, its teeth stuck outside its jaw, untidily, and its eyes were very small. Standing dripping on the cliff-top, it did not seem quite certain what to do next.

"Dinosaurs have brains in their tails as well as in their heads," Arabel told Mortimer. "I wonder what happens if ever the two brains don't agree?"

It seemed as if some such failure in transmission might be bothering this dinosaur – or perhaps it was just suffering from the confusion of someone who has been woken up too suddenly. It swung its head doubtfully, on the long, long neck, gazed for a while at the town of Glasshaven, lying below it like mustard-and-cress; paused; and finally turned inland, striding away over the grassy hills.

"Maybe we should be going after it, the creature?" said Tom Foyle the harbourmaster, a little dubiously. "The folks

at Derrycagher and Killinore may not be best pleased to have a dinosaur come lepping up the road, and they with no warning or expectation of the occurrence."

"We could give them a call on the telephone and mention that the beast is on its way?" suggested Will Byrne, Mr Plunkett's foreman.

"Very likely there's no harm at all in the beast," said another man hopefully. "For don't I recall being taught in my schooldays that dinosaurs and suchlike did all be grass-eating animals?"

"No harm in it unless it steps on your house," pointed out Mr Plunkett. "No: I am thinking we had best try to head it off. Maybe the coastguard helicopter could drop a lasso round its neck – or – or stun it with a rock."

"Some rock!"

"Maybe what's needed is some of those tranquillising darts they have in zoos," suggested Mr Jones, but not very confidently. "What the keepers use on tigers and gorillas, if they get fractious."

"Man, I doubt if there'd be enough darts in the whole of Ireland to deal with yon beast. If *he* gets fractious, heaven help us all!"

Meanwhile the whole population of Glasshaven ran up to the top of the hill, in order to see what the dinosaur would do next. And from that look-out point, everybody was relieved to see that it had not taken the road to Derrycagher and Killinore, but was walking straight inland. Every now and then it bent down the pin-sized head on the immensely long neck, and sniffed the ground.

"Acting like a bloodhound, 'tis," said Will Byrne.

"Poor thing," said Arabel suddenly. "I believe it's lonely."

And, as if in confirmation of that, the
dinosaur suddenly threw up its head and let
out a long, loud, wailing cry; such a sound as
had not echoed over the world for millions of
years. Then it went plodding on its way.

"The beast is heading for Black Feakle's
Slough," said Tom Foyle. "Maybe
somebody should warn it? 'Twould be a
shame if the only dinosaur to visit these
parts this century would go and walk into a
bog, now? And that even before Danny
O'Brien from the *Glasshaven Gazette* would be
taking its photograph?"

But he spoke too late. For while the people of Glasshaven held their breaths upon the grassy hillside, their great visitor began striding over the distant brown flatness of Black Feakle's Slough. As he went on, he sank lower and lower into the soft and oozy ground. At last his head was the only part of him visible, ploughing along like the periscope of a submarine.

Suddenly the head rose up – as if for a last look round – then it sank from view entirely.

"Well, indeed now, and that's surely rid us of an awkward problem," said Mr Plunkett, much relieved. "Come along home, now, let you, Mr and Mrs Jones and Arabel. Ye must be starving for your suppers."

So they went back to Mr Plunkett's house and ate boxsty, dillisk, stelk, frumenty, and carrageen moss, all of which were delicious. Mr Jones was still worrying about the broken glass in the factory, but Mr Plunkett said: "Ah, never give it a thought, dear man. If that darlin' child of yours hadn't had the grand notion of using the laser beam on the iceberg, there'd have been a deal more damage than that!"

"Errrk," said Mortimer sadly.

"What ails the bird?" inquired Mr Plunkett. "Does he not like the frumenty?"

"I'm afraid he's thinking about that glass with his picture on it," Arabel said. "We left it in the factory."

"He can have it this very minute," said Mr Plunkett. "I'll send the garden boy down for it directly."

And so Mortimer was able to go to bed in Mr Plunkett's coal-scuttle with the glass wrapped lovingly between his wings.

Next day the Jones family resumed their journey towards Great-aunt Rosie in Castlecoffee. But before that, they drove back with Mr Plunkett in his car to see if there were any traces remaining of the dinosaur in Black Feakle's Slough. There was none – or, only one. The bog had settled itself back into place – brown, flat, and gooey as before, like a huge plateful of molasses. But on the little rocky hill in the middle there were now *two* footprints. And a flock of Large Pink Butterflies could be seen fluttering above it.

"Maybe the dinosaur will come up again some time, Mortimer," said Arabel. "Maybe he found a friend in under there."

"Kaaark," said Mortimer. He was not really interested in the dinosaur. All he wanted was to sit gazing at the picture of himself on the glass.